for THERESA ♥

I would like to thank my marvelous models, Dana, Justin, Manny, and Melody, who were always a pleasure. I would like to thank Bonnie Burdick, Georgia Hoffman, and Candise Stiewing, three exceptional educators who shared their invaluable "I can do it myself" insight. And when it comes to collaborating, Lee Wade, Anne Schwartz, and Rachael Cole are simply the bee's knees, and for that I am very thankful.

Visit us on the Web! randomhouse.com/kids

Educators and librarians, for a variety of teaching tools, visit us at RHTeachersLibrarians.com

Library of Congress Cataloging-in-Publication Data
Fisher, Valorie.
I can do it myself / Valorie Fisher.
pages cm
ISBN 978-0-449-81593-9 (hc) — ISBN 978-0-449-81594-6 (glb)
ISBN 978-0-449-81595-3 (ebook)
1. Life skills. 2. Self-reliance. I. Title.
HQ2037.F57 2014
179'.9—dc23
2013032918

The text of this book is set in Monod Brun.
The illustrations are assemblages of dolls and toys, and a few real children, photographed with a digital camera.

MANUFACTURED IN CHINA
10 8 6 4 2 1 3 5 7
First Edition

I CAN DO IT MYSELF

VALORIE FISHER

schwartz & wade books · new york

left

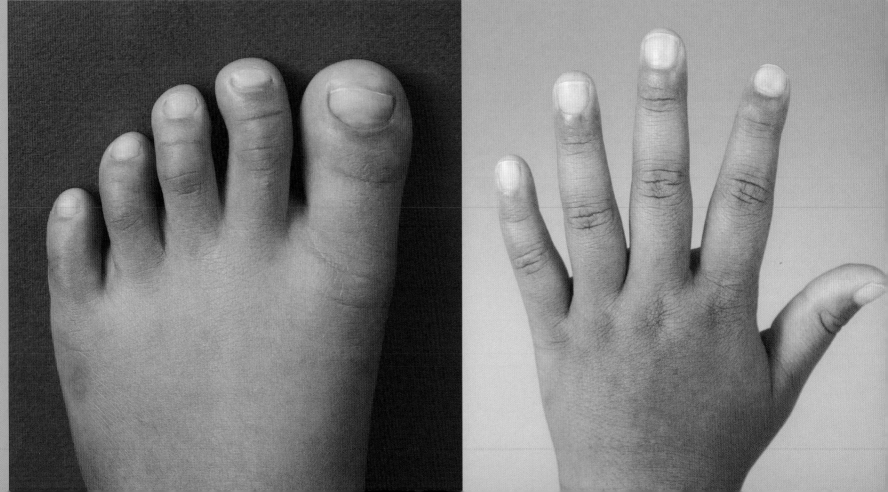

right

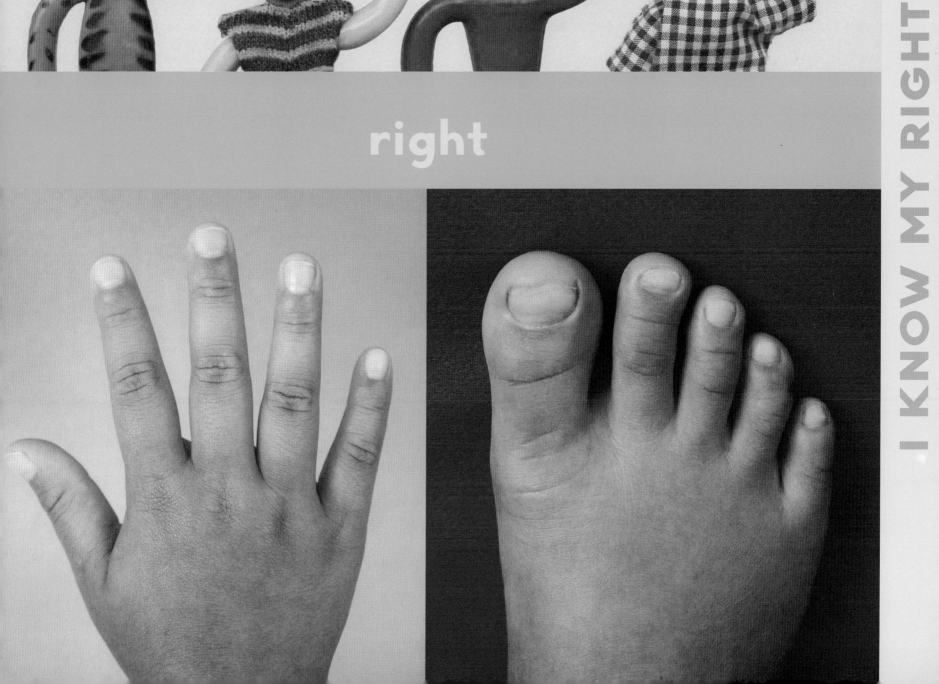

I KNOW MY RIGHT

I HOLD MY PENCIL

I write with my left hand.

Make a circle.

Make a circle.

Open the circle.

Open the circle.

Close the circle on the pencil.

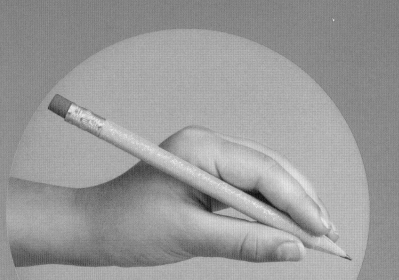

Close the circle on the pencil.

I write with my right hand.

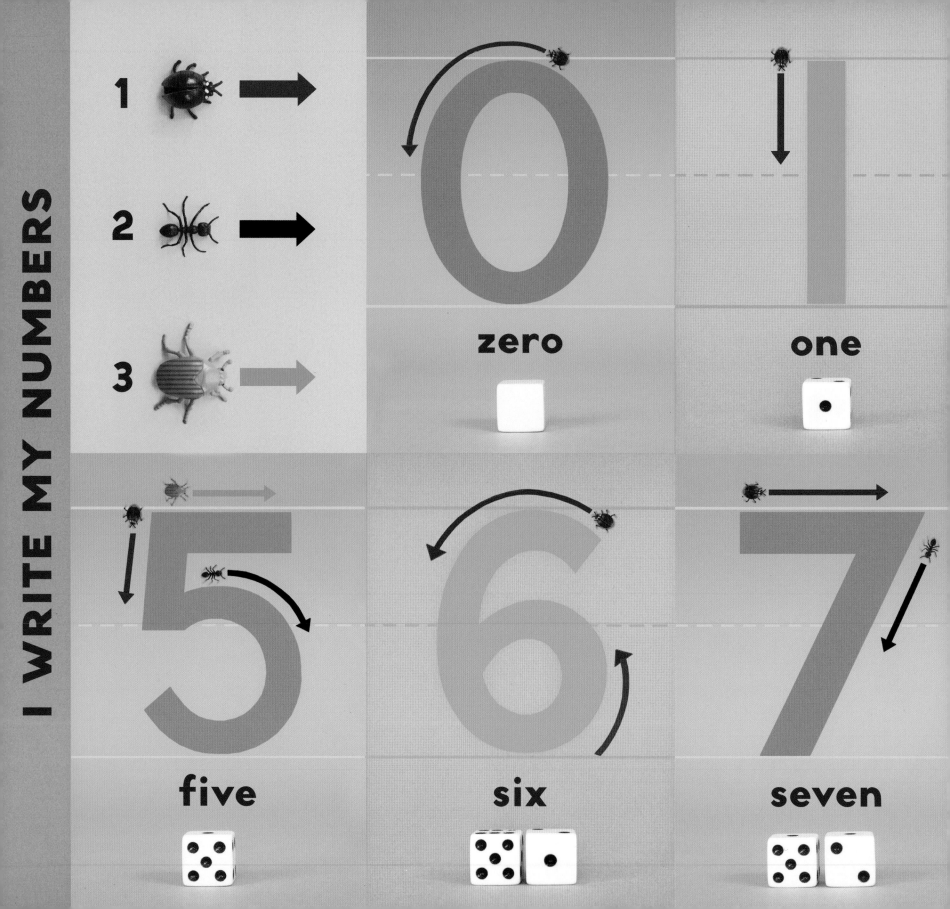

I WRITE MY NUMBERS

zero

one

five

six

seven

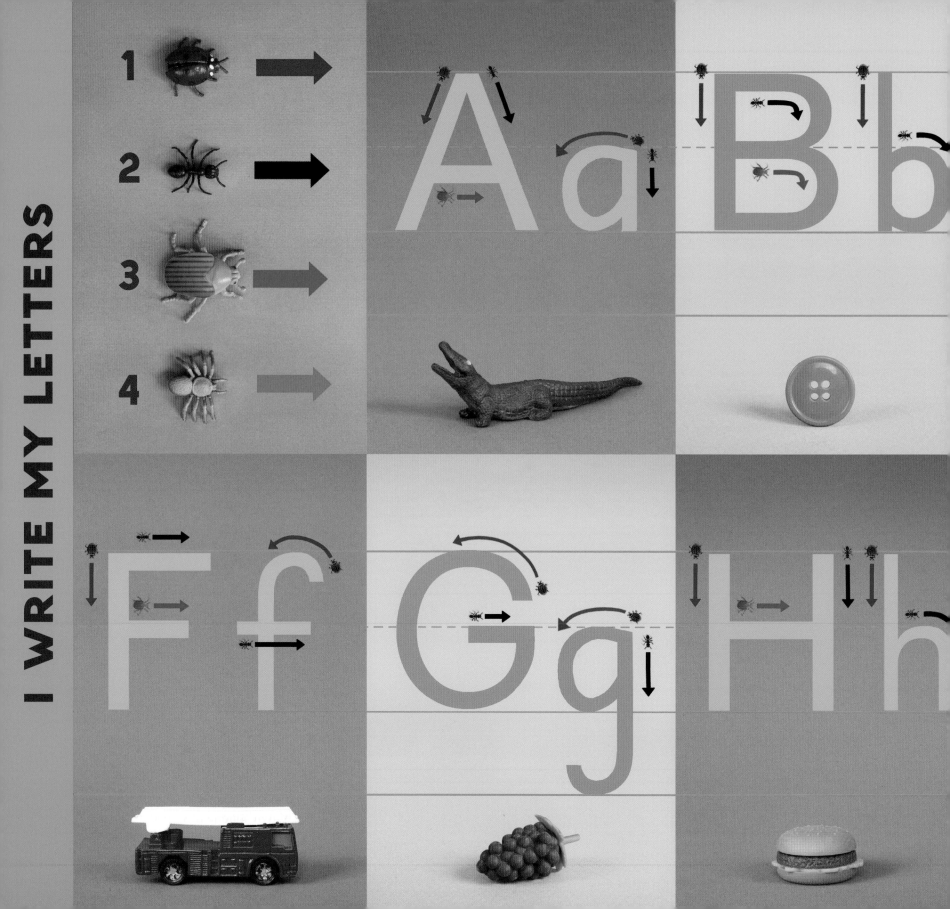

I WRITE MY LETTERS

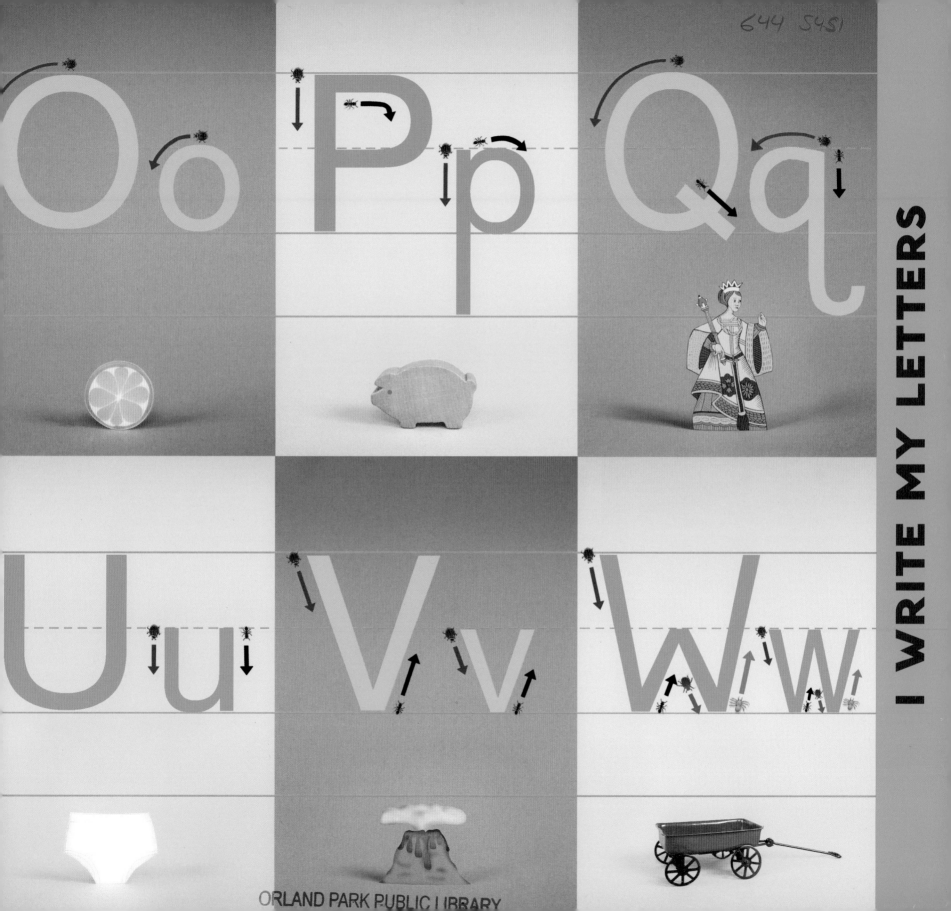

I WRITE MY LETTERS

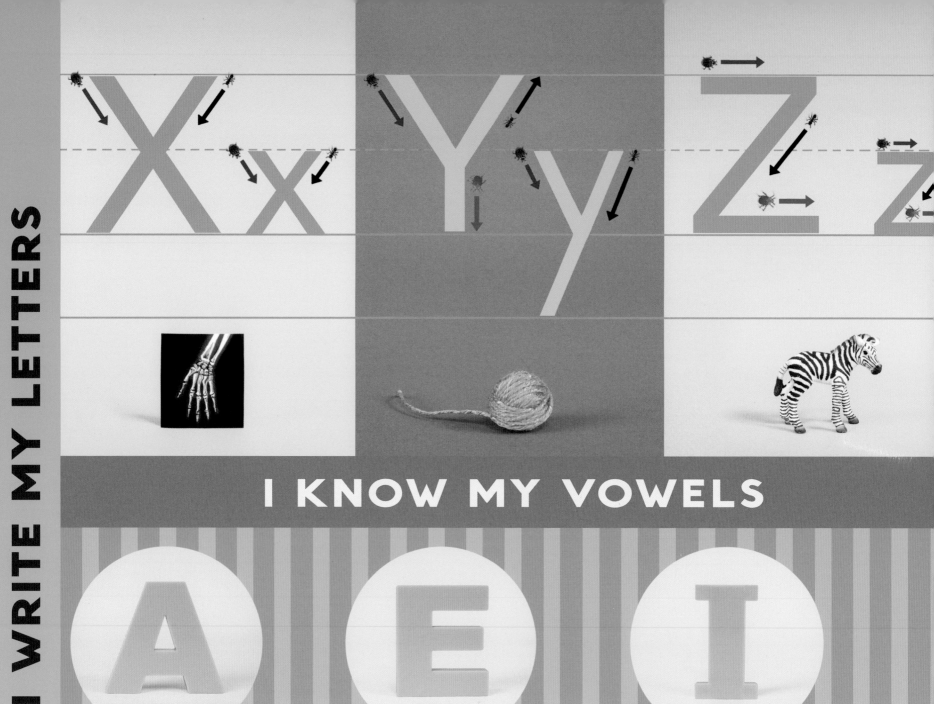

I WRITE MY LETTERS

Xx Yy Zz

I KNOW MY VOWELS

A E I
O U Y

and sometimes

frog	book	ball	cup
fish	sun	rat	pie
boot	dog	cat	shoe
hat	duck	fox	hen

hexagon

square

rectangle

trapezoid

circle

triangle

I cut carefully, holding the paper with one hand and the scissors with the other.

I USE MY SHAPES AND COLORS

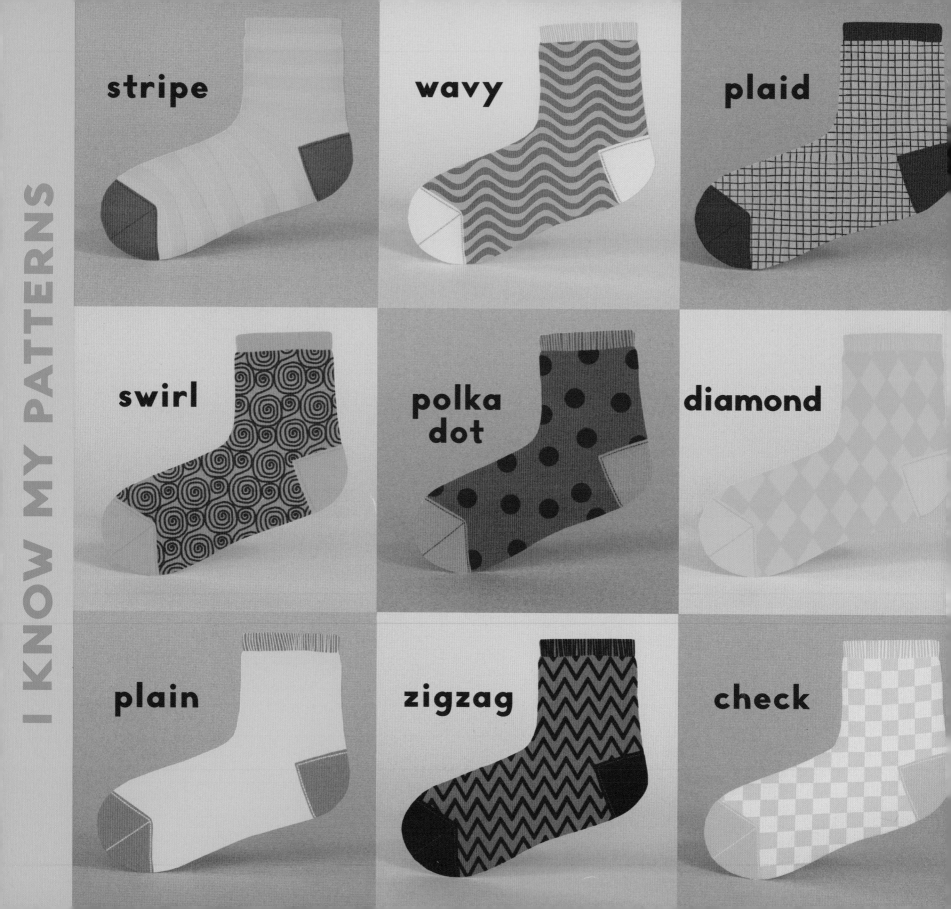

I KNOW MY PATTERNS

stripe

wavy

plaid

swirl

polka
dot

diamond

plain

zigzag

check

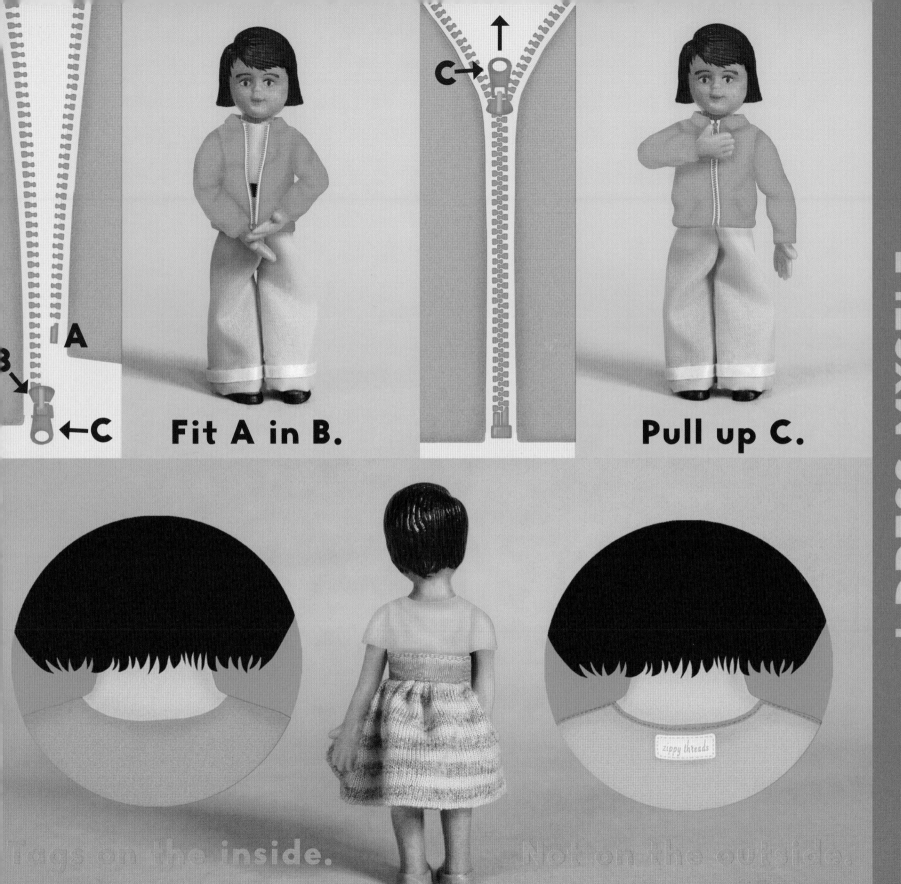

Fit A in B.

Pull up C.

I DRESS MYSELF

Tags on the inside.

Not on the outside.

I put my pants on one leg at a time.

I pull them up, then zip up and button.

I put my shirt on one sleeve at a time.

I button it   from top to bottom.

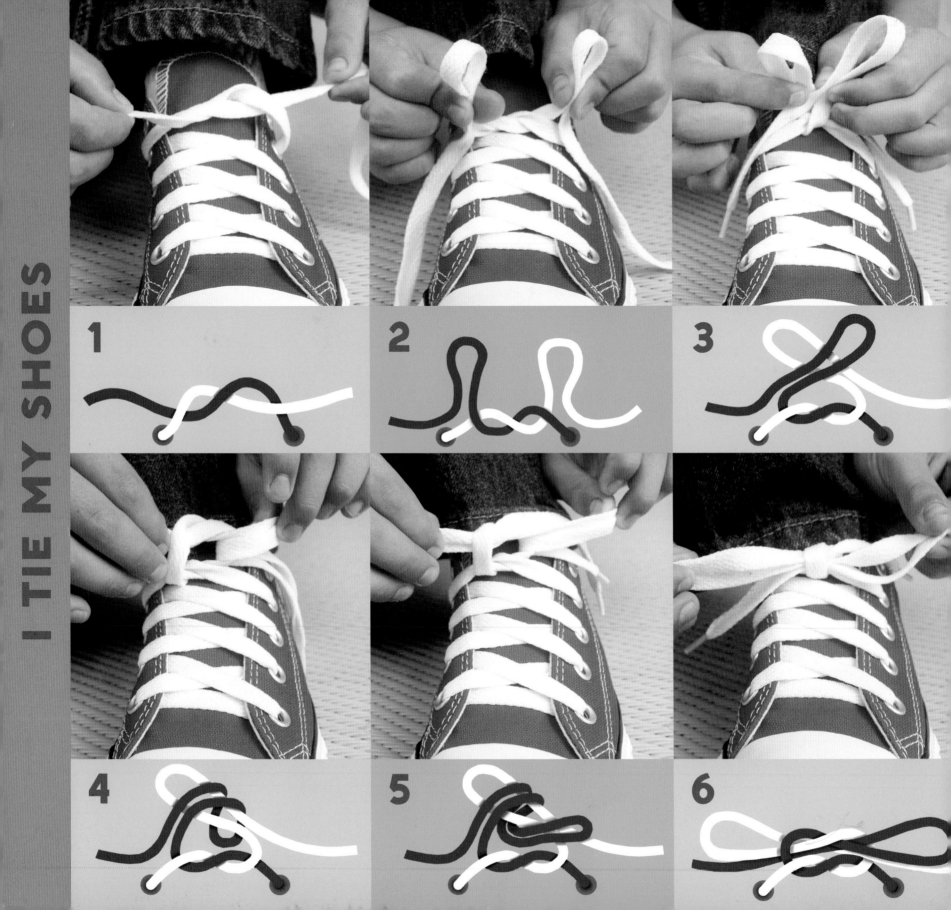

I TIE MY SHOES

1

2

3

4

5

6

I TIE MY SHOES

I BRUSH MY TEETH

I use a tiny bit of toothpaste
and brush all sides of my teeth.
Then I rinse.

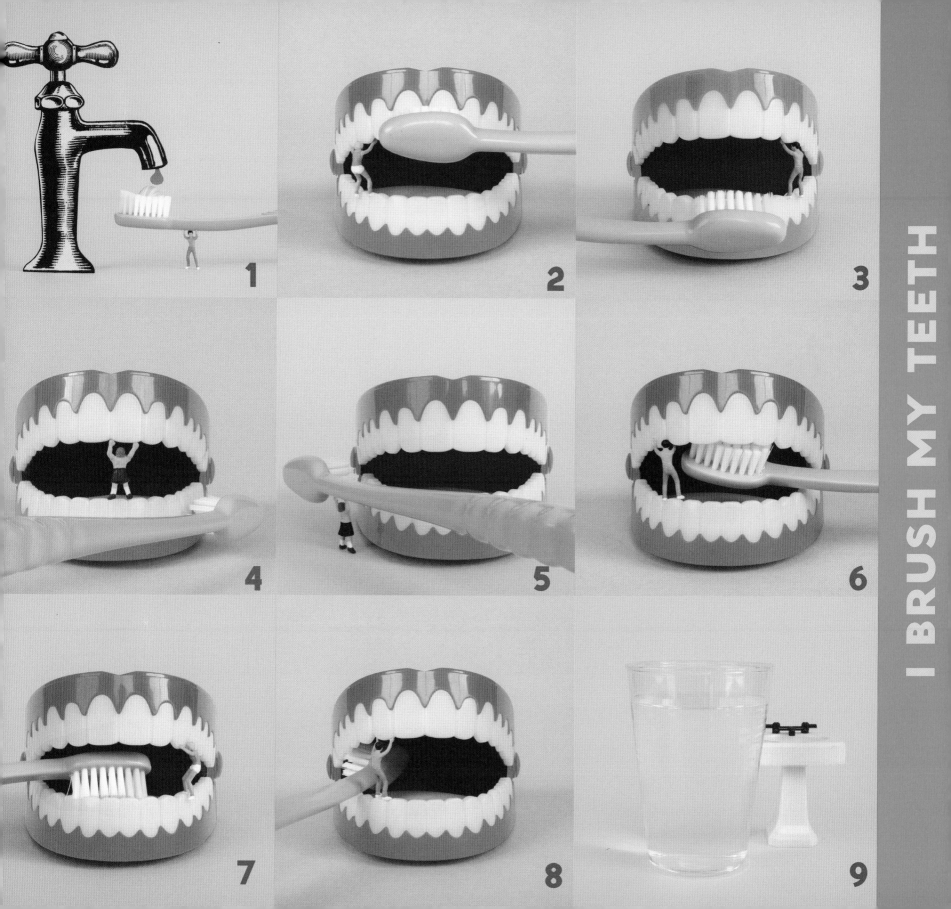

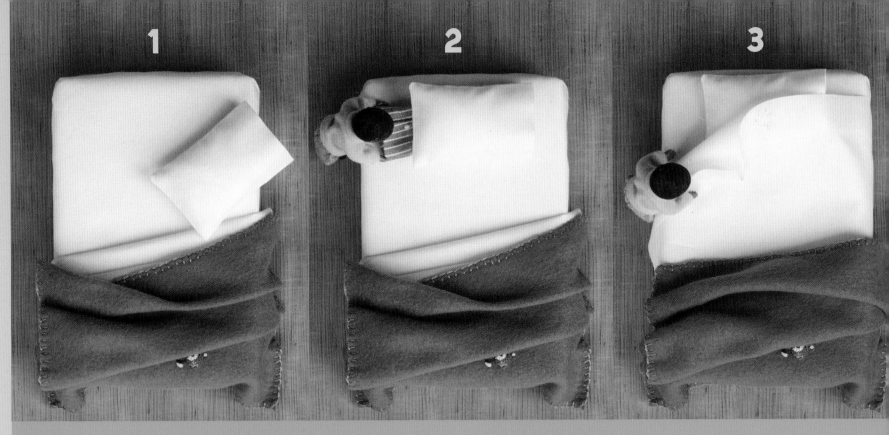

In the morning, I make my bed.

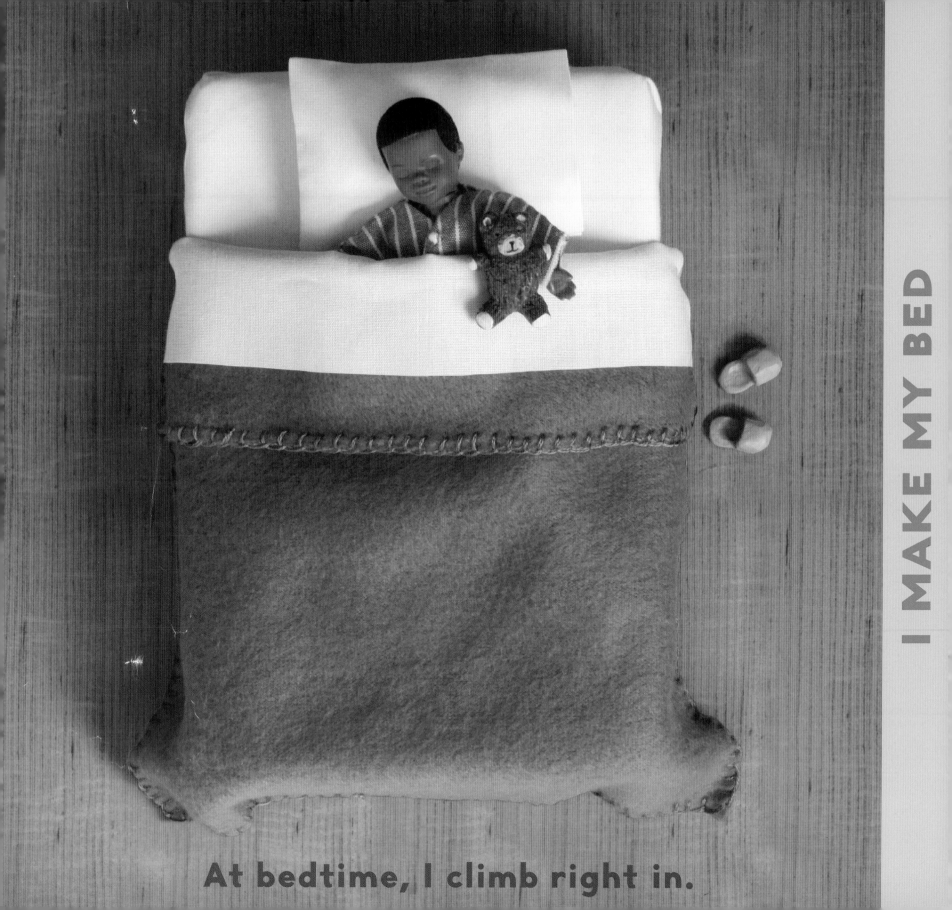

At bedtime, I climb right in.

napkin

glass

fork

plate

spoon

knife

I wash my hands before I begin.

I fold the napkins.

1

2

3

I clear my dish after the meal.

I POUR

I use two hands and
pour slowly.

I need one cup of water,
one lemon, and
one tablespoon of sugar.

I ask someone
to help me cut
the lemon.

I juice
the lemon.

I pour the water,
sugar, and lemon
juice into a glass.

I stir
until all
the sugar
dissolves.

I MAKE LEMONADE

I SAY PLEASE

please

thank you

I SAY THANK YOU